The Happy Rat Handbook

ANNETTE RAND
www.rattycorner.com

Acknowledgements

With thanks to my family for their patience and support during the many hours I spent testing these ideas, my friends for their encouragement, my rats past and present for being my inspiration, and the online rat community for those ideas that didn't spring from my own rat obsessed little brain.

ISBN-13: 978-1499150469

ISBN: 1499150466

Contents

Keep your pets safe

Please remember to keep your rats' safety in mind when using 'found' or made toys. Rats can easily get caught on loose threads, or in holes that are slightly too small for them. Discard or repair any hammocks or toys that have unsafe holes in them, or enlarge the holes to make them safe.

Welcome

*W*elcome to The Happy Rat Handbook. This book features ideas and project instructions to help you enrich and enliven your pet rats' lives, with a few ideas thrown in to make your own rat keeping life a little easier. I've been keeping pet rats since 2001. During this time I've found that I've begun to look at everything I see with the thought 'Could the rats use this?' in my head. So, if you haven't already succumbed to this mindset, I'm now going to inflict it on you as well.

I hope you enjoy these ideas and your pets enjoy their new furnishings and toys, and that you will come to forgive me for passing on my obsession.

Remember, the best entertainment for your rat is other rats. Don't keep rats on their own!

Have fun!

Fasteners & Fixings

These are just a few of the ways you can fix toys and cage furniture to the cage. I'm sure you will find others when you begin to look.

Curtain rings

Split curtain rings can be used to fasten toys to the cage bars, and to thread onto ropes to allow you to hang other toys from them. Try not to put them in the washing machine, as if they open themselves out they can do a lot of damage.

Shower curtain rings

Plastic or metal curtain rings are another useful hanging attachment. If you use the light bulb shaped rings that taper to one end, make sure the narrow end is upwards so your pet can't get trapped in the ring.

D Rings

D rings are useful attachments to sew into soft furnishings to allow you to hang them up easily. They come in many sizes, but those between 2 and 3 cm (0.8 and 1.2") are the most useful.

Keyring carabiner clips

3 cm (1.2") carabiner clips are fantastic for fixing ropes and hammocks to the cage. They're the same sort of thing you get on parrot toys for hanging them up. The cheaper versions may be slightly rust prone, but my solution is to keep them in a jar with a little oil when I'm not using them.

Dog lead trigger clips

These clips are useful for clipping cage doors closed when your pet has learned to open them, and also for hanging toys that you want to be able to rotate.

Chain

Lengths of chain can turn a hammock into a swing or stacking hammock, hang up a tube, or help a toy hang down into the best place for your pets to reach it. The most useful weight is that used for sink plugs or a little heavier.

Making holes in plastic

Some of the ideas in this book ask you to make holes in plastic items. The two simplest ways are to drill the hole in the proper manner, or to melt a hole with a soldering iron. If you're going to use this second way, be very careful not to let it drip hot plastic onto work surfaces, or onto you, remember to turn off the iron when you've done, and please bear in mind it will need a lot of cleaning before re-use for soldering.

Plastic needlepoint canvas

This is fantastic stuff for adding stiffness to fabric toys. It drains, it doesn't break the washing machine, and it's easy to sew through to strengthen the layers.

Nuts and bolts

Sets of nuts, bolts and washers are really handy for fixing things such as litter trays onto cage bars. You'll need some nice big washers, at least 2 cm (0.8") diameter, but as long as the bolts go through the bars the thickness isn't that important.

Cable ties/zip ties

These are useful for semi-permanent fixtures, although you may find that they are regarded as particularly tasty snacks.

Hose clips

A more permanent metal version of the cable ties.

Fixing strips

This is an alternative to using cord or webbing to attach fixings to hammocks, or to hang things up with. The finished strip is about a quarter (a fourth) the width of the fabric strip you began with. Make more than you need so you can cut pieces to length when you need them.

You will need

- A strip of fabric 6 cm (2.4") or more wide.

Step by step

1. Fold both of the edges in towards the centre so they meet.

2. Fold the strip in half again.

3. Sew along the open edge.

4. Sew along the second edge.

Pet safe glue

This recipe makes a thin glue suitable for making papier mâché toys. For a thicker glue to fix boxes and suchlike together, double up on the flour (or halve the quantity of water).

You will need

- 1 heaped tablespoon of flour
- Water

Step by step

1. Boil 500ml (17 fl oz) of water in a saucepan.

2. Mix the sieved flour with 100ml (3 fl oz) cold water. Mix to a smooth consistency.

3. When completely free of lumps, add the mixture to the water in the saucepan.

4. Gently boil, **stirring constantly** for two or three minutes until the mixture thickens.

5. Allow to cool before using. (You can sieve it if it's gone lumpy.)

6. Store in an airtight container.

Fun Foods

Food as a game is appreciated by most rats, although you do have to remember to feed any single food in moderation and to count it as part of their daily allowance.

Don't overfeed

It's not a kindness to overfeed your rats. If you 'free feed' an unlimited amount of food they can become obese and inactive, getting so much less out of life. Make sure your rats have plenty of climbing opportunities and don't top up their food throughout the day. If you have rats who need to gain weight living with those who need to lose it, let the thinner rats go home first to feed before their sturdier cagemates go in.

Dry mix

The first choice here is between a muesli type mix, and a homogenous pelleted mix. The reasoning behind pellets, nuggets or lab blocks is that they provide a balanced diet and prevent picking. The flaw in this reasoning is that every brand of block provides a differently balanced diet, some containing far more fat or protein than may be ideal for your pet rats. These diets are also often based on the needs of lab rats, which generally live a far more restricted and less active life than a pet rat.

I also feel that feeding pellets is missing a trick enrichment-wise. My preference is to feed a mixed muesli type diet, as rats naturally eat a wide variety of foods, unlike rabbits, for example, which naturally have a diet based on one main ingredient.

There are many shop bought mixes to choose from, with varying degrees of quality and processing. The advantage we have with keeping rats is that they are very resilient and have no problem with switching from one brand to another, so feeding a rotation of different brands can help to even out the differences. Alternatively you can feed rabbit muesli as a base and add animal protein of your own choice, rather than the often poor quality meat products added to commercial rat mix.

There is also a growing trend for feeding 'straights', or unprocessed grains, as a base for a home mix, plus a small amount of animal protein and plenty of fresh foods. If you want to try this approach, you need to watch the levels of calcium, copper and vitamin D, as these are the most difficult areas to cover in a home made mix and will probably need supplementing.

Scatter feeding

The very easiest game to play with rats and their food is to scatter their dry mix around the cage so they have to look for it. If your rats have always had their food in a bowl, it may take them a little while to work out what they have to do. You can begin by giving their mix in a pile on their substrate, then spread it further and mix it in more as the days go by.

Fruit

Many fruits are accepted happily by rats. Banana is the one I've found to be a particular favourite, complete with the skin, but apple, cherries, grapes, plums, melons, strawberries and other berries are also generally well received. Feeding rats red fruit can result in the cage looking as if a massacre has taken place, so remember to warn your family beforehand!

Be aware that fruit pits (stones) are often toxic, so need to be removed before giving the fruit to the rats, or taken out as soon as they are uncovered.

Greens

Green leaves such as kale, spring greens, broccoli and pak choi are really good for your rats, and can be chopped up and stuffed into small boxes or toilet roll tubes so they have to be pulled out. Cut some fruit and veg up into small pieces and mix that in too if you like. You can also buy small metal basket hangers to stuff with greens, or small logs with holes intended for hamsters to run through.

Plants

You may have found out how difficult it is to keep your rats away from houseplants that they shouldn't eat. How about giving them something they can eat? Plant up a pot or two of tasty foods like basil, parsley, dandelion, nasturtium and cat grass in some sterilised compost or soil (baked). You can even buy packets of edible plant seeds 'for your rabbit or tortoise' online. As usual, the reaction varies from rat to rat. The whole pot full may be destroyed at one sitting, in which case you'll be glad you made a second pot, or your rats may prefer to graze a little at a time.

Corn cob

Corn on the cob, or sweetcorn, is adored by rats. It's often included as a dried ingredient in mixes, but a fresh corn cob takes it to a new level in a rat's opinion. Although it's quite heavy for a rat, they will attempt to drag it away to stash it. You can stop this by hanging it up with a piece of string.

You could also try hanging up other pieces of fruit and veg such as apple or carrot, either tying string around it or boring a hole through with a skewer. Watch to see if one of your rats works out that they can chew through the string to get the prize.

Pea fishing

There seem to be as many ways to set up pea fishing as there are rat owners. The basic idea is to add fresh or frozen peas to water, and let the rats fish for them. I've tried other vegetables, but peas seem to be the best because not only do the ratties love them, but also some peas will float and some will sink. The reaction from the rats is as individual as everything else they do. Some will love the game, some will be confused, some will perch on the edge and fish in a genteel fashion while others will dive right in, and some will wait until another rat has retrieved a pea before grabbing it and scampering away.

At its simplest, this is just a case of putting some peas in an old saucepan and adding water. The handle makes a good perch, but it's a stretch to reach the peas.

My favourite setup is to take a fairly shallow plastic storage box, cage base or clean cat litter tray, put a rock in one corner for the rats to stand on, add some clean pebbles and sea shells, and then add the peas. You can prop up one end of the box to make a shallow end and a deep end, but if you can find the right bit of shallow sloping rock that will do the same job.

Some rats will enjoy deep pea diving. This involves a deeper container with a ramp or ladder into it, and a gradual increase in depth over several sessions.

Eggs

Scrambled eggs make a great ratty treat, but here we're looking at boiled eggs. These are a challenge to get into, but also roll so beautifully that you can have something resembling a ratty rugger match while they are trying to gain entrance and squabbling over possession. If your rats lose interest, tap the egg on something hard to make a small crack; this will let them smell the prize and help them to get inside.

The rats will eat the shell as well, so there is very little clearing up to do.

Pumpkin

Pumpkin is safe for rats to eat, and is fun to hollow out to let the rats inside. They will also enjoy the seeds, which can be eaten fresh or dried for later. Smaller squashes can be given whole as an exercise in excavation.

This is the opportunity to get some fun Halloween photos of ratties inside your jack-o'-lantern.

Bones

Cooked bones are safe for your rats to eat, as they gnaw the bone into dust rather than crunching on it. A whole chicken carcase will result in some very happy, but rather greasy, little rats. Smaller bones will become the focus of chases and tug-of-wars. Bones are also a useful size for hanging up to encourage your rats to share a little more.

Nuts

Nuts in their shells are a readymade activity for your rats. Walnut, brazil, pecan, almond, hazelnut and sweet chestnut are some of those suitable for ratties, with varying degrees of difficulty in getting inside.

Millet

Millet sprays sold for birds are a fun food to hang in your cage, preferably in a place where it's difficult, but not impossible, to reach. You can also buy wheat and other grain stalks for pets, but I would be wary of picking any from the field unless you are completely sure it's not been sprayed with pesticides recently.

A loaf of bread

If you have a slightly stale loaf, or just want to give your ratties some fun, try giving them an unsliced loaf. Start a burrow into the middle for them and they will continue to excavate, briefly giving them a bread house before they complete the demolition. If the weather is warm, try freezing the loaf after starting the burrow to give them an extra challenge. A loaf will feed a large number of rats, so if they don't finish it be sure to remove any bread that starts to go mouldy.

Bowl stacker

A quick idea to make your own life a little easier: The commonly found Mason Cash pet bowls don't stack at all well, but they do fit very nicely into a toilet roll holder for storage.

Digging & Diving

Digging is a natural occupation for rats, but something they don't get much opportunity for in most cages.

Stones and shells

Fill a box with some shiny stones or some shells to give them something interesting to rummage through. You can hide a small amount of food in the box if you like, but they will probably investigate without this encouragement. Shells may get nibbled, but this is not a problem.

Shredded paper

Cross shredded paper can be fun if you put it into a bowl or box, especially if you involve food and mix in some puffed rice. Pack shredded paper into a small box to encourage your ratties to pull it out, or into a large box for rummaging and exploring in. Do make sure the edges of the paper aren't sharp, as this can cut the rats' feet.

Compost digging box

A box of sterilised soil or compost will give your ratties a nicely messy place to dig and play in, especially if you mix some small seeds in for them to find. The bonus is that any seeds that are missed will grow into shoots, which are even more tasty.

Cat grass

Cat grass is sometimes sold in small containers to grow for your pet cat, but even more useful is a packet of seed. Grow this in your digging box before letting your ratties loose on it. As covered in the previous chapter, there's no reason to restrict yourself to just grass; any other edible plant seed can be added.

Wrapping paper box

What do you do with all your used wrapping paper? Give it to your rats, of course! A big cardboard box of scrunched up paper, with maybe a hole near the bottom to let them pull the paper out through, will give you and your ratties a fun hour or two of entertainment.

Blankie mountain

Make a mountain out of an old, unwanted blanket. Your rats will have lots of fun burrowing and hiding, and possibly sleeping in there as well. Don't walk over it unless you are sure you know where all your rats are!

Water

Give your rats a bowl of water while they're out. They'll use it to drink from, but if it's just that bit bigger they're likely to get into it too, especially if you float some chew sticks or wooden blocks in it.

Snow

Our rats don't get to experience the outside world very often. Let them share in the excitement of a snowy day by bringing in a tray of snow for them to explore.

Shredding & Stashing

Rats love paper. Shredded paper, newspaper, tissue paper, your homework, the book you're reading, even your paper money. Cloth is good too; your clothes, your curtains, your furniture. Why not channel this into some fun and games? It won't stop them chewing the things you don't want them to, but it will entertain them and make them happy.

Paper bags

Put their dry mix into a paper bag and twist the top closed, or machine sew it up.

Phone book

Use up your old phone book by tearing out a few pages, cutting the pages into four or five strips almost to the top, and hanging it outside their cage so they have to pull the pieces in.

Hay rack

Put a rabbit hay rack on the outside of the cage full of tissue paper to pull in, or even be traditional and put hay in it.

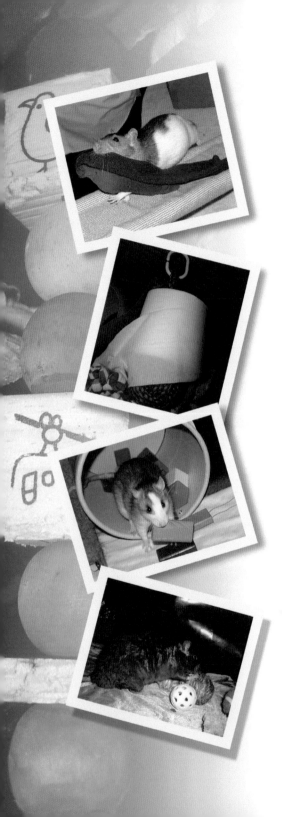

Old socks

Make a sock dispenser for your old socks; seal them up inside a box and make a small hole to pull the socks out through, or stuff them into a tube and hang it in the cage.

Crackers

Make crackers for your rats by filling a tissue covered toilet roll tube with pasta, nuts and treats and wrapping it in tissue or paper towel, with a small piece of string to seal the ends.

Piñata

Hang your rat crackers up to make a ratty piñata.

Toilet rolls

Don't just give your rats the toilet roll tube, give them the whole roll. Hang up cheap toilet rolls by threading them onto ropes or branches, or on a parrot toy or dog toy.

Children's building blocks & beads

Don't ask me why, but wooden building blocks are very stashable, as are chunky wooden beads. Beads can also be threaded onto chains to make chew toys to hang in your rats' cage.

Balls

Some ratties enjoy small balls sold as cat toys, especially the sort with holes that you can put food inside. You can also make your own treat ball with kitchen roll or toilet roll tube. If you like, you can make it more of a challenge by gluing it together with pet safe glue (see page 6).

You will need

- 1 toilet roll tube or kitchen roll tube
- 1 or more small treats

Step by Step

1. Cut the tube into rings about 2cm (0.8") across.
2. Cross over two of the rings, and put the treat(s) inside.
3. Put another ring around the first two.

Corks

Wine corks are very interesting, particularly if they still smell of wine. They do, however, get chewed into a pile of small pieces after a short time.

Feathers

There's something about feathers that rats can't resist. This is why it's not a good idea to let your rats meet your pet bird. Any safe cat toy that includes feathers, such as feather wands and balls with feathers attached, will be very much enjoyed. If you want to give your rats 'found' feathers, give the feathers a zap in the microwave (alongside a cup of water), just to make sure you're not bringing in any mites or similar.

Ice cube fishing

A bowl of ice cubes in water goes down surprisingly well, but they are a source of great puzzlement to ratties. Stashable, but difficult to handle and they disappear leaving just a strange damp patch behind. A very funny game to watch.

A wotnot box

Make a box or bowl of any bits and pieces that look interesting and safe for your rats to explore. Blocks, beads, pebbles, shells, wooden chew sticks, nuts, cork. Add some water for a change, so that some of the toys float and others don't.

Wooden parrot toys

There are an amazing variety of parrot toys available that make decorative and chewable toys for rats. Prices vary widely, so shop around before you buy.

Climbing & Swinging

Climbing is a natural and healthy activity for rats, who will love the opportunity to clamber around both in their cage and at playtime. Rats are also surprisingly willing to step onto an unstable surface, so I've included some swinging toys in this section.

Wine rack

Wooden wine racks make the best climbing frames you could think of, and usefully tend to come flat packed so you can get creative with the layout. They can be set either way up, to give square or diamond shaped arrangements. Be careful not to leave any overhangs, as it's a sure thing that your ratties will all decide to sit on the overhang at the same time and tip the rack over.

Fold out wine racks need to be used with care and attached to the side of the cage or something equally solid and stable, so that there is no possibility of them folding up with rats inside.

Ramps and ladders

Ramps and ladders are mostly useful for helping older and less agile ratties to make more use of the cage levels, although they can be a good way of letting your rats have safe access to their cage during playtime. You can make an elongated version of the plain and simple hammock shown on page 31 to serve as a fabric ramp.

19

Plastic baskets

You can often find small plastic storage baskets for a very low price. Check that there are no holes which narrow as they go down, as these could be a foot trapping hazard. Then either put fixings through holes that are already there, or make some holes to fix them through, and hang it up with some equal lengths of chain. You can fix it at two ends, which will make it very 'tippy', or put a fixing at one end and two fixings on the sides towards the other end. A basket with a handle could be hung from the centre of the handle, making it even more of a swing.

Plastic plate swing

Make three or four holes around the edge of a plastic plate and attach a chain to each hole, hanging them from a single point above.

Plant pot swing

Find a strong and colourful plastic plant pot to turn into a swing with ready-made drainage holes.

Hammock swing

Use chains as extensions to hang a hammock from the top of the cage, with the corners closer together than usual or even with all four chains hung from a single point.

Parrot perches

There is a wide selection of parrot perches and branches that will make fun and safe cage accessories for your rats. Use them to make a retreat high up in the top of the cage, a perch to come out of the door, or use several to make steps up the side of the cage.

Wardrobe organiser

These organisers from Ikea make a fantastic climbing toy. They are made from plastic rings with cord looped around them. Carefully cut off the coat hanger piece and hang them across the cage, making a safety net or a sloped cargo net. The cord will get chewed, so you will need to check for and remove loose ends regularly. Clean by scrubbing (I've found from experience that they will get caught in the seal of the washing machine door). You can re-cover the rings by knotting string around them if you have the patience, or use the hoops when making other rat toys, for example for holding the ends of tunnels open.

Branches

Adding branches to your ratties' cage will give them hours of fun. It's not a good idea if your rats are nervous and hard to catch, as it will reduce your access and give them a lot of scope for avoiding your hand. Any branch that goes into your cage should be soaked and scrubbed, frozen, or baked to make sure there are no bugs hiding in there. Some of the safe woods are apple, crab apple, pear, beech, birch, willow, magnolia, and also hawthorn and bramble, which will need the thorns stripping off first.

Ropes

Your rats will enjoy a rope stretched across their cage, or you can hang one vertically from the top if you have a tall cage. Use D rings or curtain rings threaded onto the rope to zigzag it across the cage, anchor the corner of hammocks, or to hang toys from. Make a 'ladder' up one corner of the cage by zig-zagging the rope back and forth across the corner.

Bought rope

A length of thick rope (or even an unwanted judo belt) can very easily be turned into a toy for your rats, simply by knotting one end, threading some rings onto it and knotting the final end.

Plaited paper rope

You will need

- Three sheets of newspaper
- Cable ties or string
- Clips to attach to the cage

Step by step

1. Take three full sheets of newspaper, and roll each sheet lengthways to make three thin strips of paper.

2. Twist each strip as tightly as you can.

22

3. Secure one end with a cable tie and plait the three strips together.

4. Bring the end to meet the beginning, and fix them together with a cable tie, or leave it as a straight strip and fix across the corner of a cage.

5. Extend the ropes by gluing more sheets of newspaper together before beginning (see pet safe glue on page 6), or use the wonderfully long lengths of packing paper that come in some parcels.

Making ropes from bed sheets

This makes a strong plaited rope that can be machine washed, albeit a little noisily.

You will need

- D rings or curtain rings, 20 to 30 mm (0.8 to 1.2")
- An old sheet

Step by step

1. First you need to work out what size your old sheet is and how many ropes you want to make. The more ropes you make from a sheet, the thinner the finished rope will be. Single sheets will make two or three ropes and double or king size sheets will make three or four ropes.

2. Your sheet will probably have wide hems at the top and bottom, and sides with only a small hem. Cut or tear your sheet into the number of ropes you've decided on, starting with a cut through one of the wide hems. The strips don't need to be exactly the same size; it's fun to have different thicknesses of rope.

3. For each rope, take one of the strips and cut it into three approximately equal smaller strips. (If you're using the same sheet for all three strips, you can leave the second hem uncut so the three strips are still attached.)

4. It makes it easier to handle if you gather the pieces into elastic bands at this stage, but that's optional.

5. Use an elastic band or some string to hold the three ends together.

6. At the other end, thread a D ring onto one or two of the three pieces, and push up to the end with the elastic band.

7. Plait the three strips together as tightly as you can, twisting each one in the same direction as you go along to compact and strengthen the strips and adding another ring about every 20 cm (8").

8. For added security, put a few stitches in each end to stop it coming untied in the wash. Machine sewing will probably hold better, but hand sewing will still help.

9. Tie a knot in each end, over the plaiting and the end D rings.

10. Adjust the rope's length by tying more knots in it.

Balance pole or climbing pole

You will need

- A strong postage tube, slightly longer/ wider than your rats' cage.
- Thin rough rope/thick string such as sisal, hemp or coir, length depending on the size of the tube (I used a 30 metre pack of coir garden rope).
- Pet safe glue (see page 6)

Step by step

1. Take any lids or ends off the posting tube, and cut two slots in each end, lined up with each other.

2. Cut your rope in half.

3. Tie a knot in one end of one piece of rope, and slide it into one of the slots on the tube, with the knot inside.

4. Wind the rope around the tube. It doesn't need to be evenly spaced, and you don't want it packed tight because we're going to add a second strand later. Leave at least a rope's width between each winding.

5. At the other end, tie a knot approximately next to one of the slots, and force the knot into the slot.

6. Paint a line of glue between the coils of rope, all the way along the tube. This will space the rope out more evenly ready for the next step.

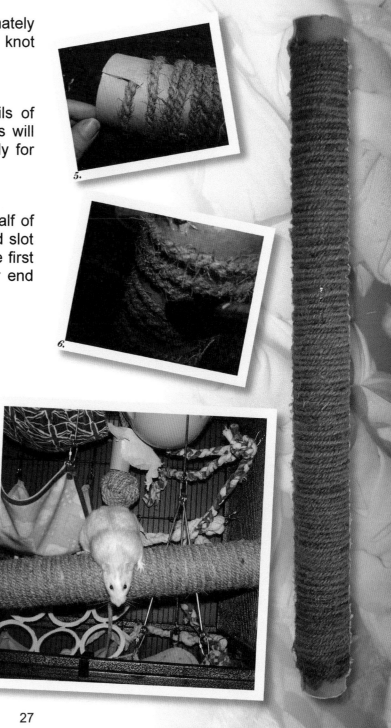

7. Tie a knot in the end of the second half of the rope and slide this into the second slot at one end. Wind it along between the first half of the rope, and finish at the far end with a knot again.

8. Leave the tube to dry.

9. Cut some more slots in the ends so they will slide onto the bars of the cage, and wedge the tube in place, either across the cage to make a balance pole, or between the ceiling and base of the cage to make a climbing pole.

Hammocks

Rats love to lounge and loaf high up in the cage, and also occasionally need a safety net lower down when they misjudge a leap, so hammocks are a very useful addition to their cage.

The tea towel

Take a cheap or old tea towel or pillow case. Fold it in half if it's too big for your cage. Make a hole in each corner and clip it to the cage with a curtain ring or carabiner clip.

The simple jeans leg

When your jeans are too far gone to wear any longer, cut the legs off to hammock length, and thread onto chains or bird perches to suspend across the cage. Fix the chains/perches close together for a tube type hammock, or further apart for a shelf type. (You can finish the edges of the cloth if you like - frayed edges can form dangerous loops when you wash them, so this saves having to trim them.)

The jeans seat

When you've cut off the legs take the remaining top piece and sew across the leg holes to make a large pocket. Attach one side to the side or top of the cage using the belt loops.

The old hat

Your old beanie hat will make a lovely snuggle pocket to fix to the side of the cage.

Sweatshirts

Use up old or outgrown school uniform sweatshirts, or tatty old tops you no longer wear. These make wonderful hammocks. Just add four fixings and hang them up, or put extra clips on the arms to make tunnels to different levels.

Old handbags

Recycle your old handbags and shoulder bags by attaching them to the cage as vertical pocket hammocks. Make sure there is nowhere the rats could trap or injure themselves.

Just about anything you can think of

What is says. If there's a way to hang it up and it doesn't have any potential hazards then it's a hammock. T-shirts, bras, Y fronts; if it's doable then someone has already done it. Just ask the Internet.

Machine sewn hammocks

Here are instructions for some machine sewn hammocks that may last a little longer than the shop bought ones, but there are no guarantees with ratties. Some suitable materials are sweatshirt type fleece, strong curtain fabrics and close weave fabric. Fluffy fabrics look nice, but don't last.

Plain and simple hammock

Although this is very simple to make, it can be turned into a double hammock simply by making two of slightly different sizes, and hanging them with the smaller above the larger on the same fixings so your rats can get in around the edges.

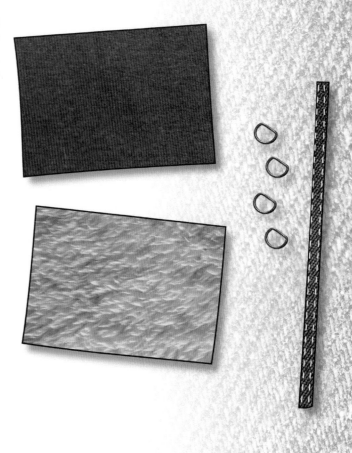

You will need

- 2 pieces of fabric about 2 or 3 cm (0.8 to 1.2") larger in each direction than you want the finished hammock to be. You can add more layers of fabric if you want to make it stronger.
- 40 cm (16") of fixing strip (see page 5)
- 4 x D rings

Step by step

1. Cut four pieces of fixing strip, each about 10 cm (4") long, and thread a D ring onto each strip.

2. Place one piece of fabric right side up and place the fixing strips on the shorter sides 3 or 4 cm (1.2 to 1.8") from the corners, so that about 1 cm (0.4") of the strip shows.

1.

3. Sew across the ends to hold the strips in place.

4. Put the second piece of fabric on top, right side down, and sew around the edges about 1 to 1.5 cm (0.4 to 0.6") from the edge, leaving a 8 to 10 cm (3 to 4") gap to let you turn the hammock right side out.

5. Trim the seam across at the corners.

6. Turn the hammock right side out through the hole and hand sew the hole together.

7. Stitch around the edges and then sew the two layers together to make the hammock more chew resistant.

Pocket hammock

This gives your rats a cosy place to hide, without making their own entrance into the inside of the hammock.

You will need

- 2 pieces of fabric about 3 cm (1.2") wider than you want the finished hammock to be, and a little less than twice as long.
- 40 cm (16") of fixing strip (see page 5).
- 4 x D rings

Step by step

1. Cut four pieces of fixing strip, each about 10 cm (4") long, and thread a D ring onto each strip.

2. Place one of the pieces of fabric right side up and place the fixing strips on the longer sides. Two of them go about 4 cm (1.5") from the corners at one end, and the other two about halfway along, so that about 1 cm (0.4") of the strip shows. Sew across the edge to hold them in place.

3. Put the second piece of fabric on top, right side down.

4. Sew around the edges about 1.5 cm (0.5") from the edge, leaving a 8 to 10 cm (3 to 4") gap unsewn to let you turn the hammock right side out.

5. Trim the seam across the corners.

6. Turn the hammock right side out and hand sew the hole together.

7. Stitch around the edges and then sew over the two layers to quilt them together and make the hammock more chew resistant.

8. Fold back the end with no fixings, to form the pocket.

9. Sew along the sides to make the edges of the pocket.

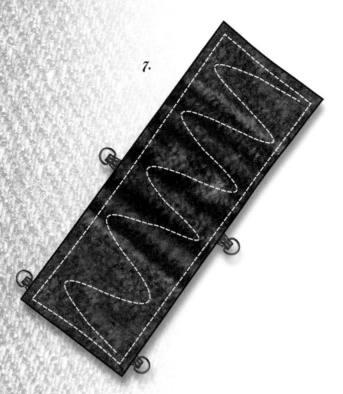

7.

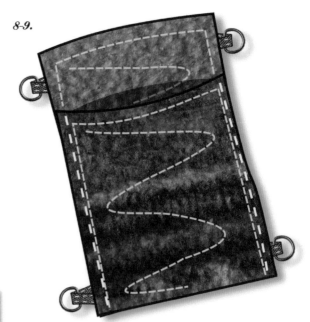

8-9.

Repair and re-use
When your rats' hammocks get chewed and tatty, don't throw them away. They can be given a second lease of life by pairing up similar sized hammocks so that there's at least one fixing left at each corner and sewing them together to make new, thicker hammocks.

Huts & Hidey Holes

Every rat needs a hidey hole; somewhere to feel safe and protected. In fact, most cages come with a house of some sort. But ratties love variety and choice, so here are a few ways to give them that.

Boxes

The most simple and cheapest way to give your rats a shelter is to provide cardboard boxes. A small box with a simple entrance hole, a fairytale castle of cardboard, or a mighty 3D maze. Your rats will, of course, redesign their shelter to add extra doors and extra odour, but when it becomes too 'ratty' it can be exchanged for a new one to begin the process again.

Food sacks

Because I have a lot of rats, I buy their food in large food sacks, made of paper. These are a fantastic, rustly experience, and work best with a tunnel in the entrance to hold them open, and maybe a bottom corner torn off to allow another exit.

Chicken feeder hut

There are some chicken feeders available that look just like little huts with windows all around. In fact, they are little huts with windows all around, just ask the rats.

Bolt on plant pot

Bolt a colourful plant pot onto the side of the cage, using a nut and bolt and a couple of big washers to fix it through the drainage holes. Make sure you can get at the fixings to remove the pot for washing, because it will get stained.

Cat trees

Cat trees make great climbing toys, but with places to lurk during playtime. Don't spend a fortune on them, as they will get soiled over time.

Dolls' house

As much for you as for the rats; give them a sturdy dolls' house to play in. I found a cheap wooden one second hand on a market stall and painted it up to help keep it clean.

Toy boat/car

I don't know what the rats think, but I think they look cute sitting in a chunky toy car.

Wall planter

These come with a ready made hole for you to bolt or cable tie them to the cage.

Climb-N-Sail Ferret Boat

This SuperPet toy gets a special mention because it's the most durable rat toy I've had. It's lasted well over a decade and it's still being played with.

Savic Sputnik XL

These are purpose made rat houses, but they are so well loved that they deserve a mention. They can stand on the cage floor, or hang from the ceiling of the cage. The fixings provided don't reliably hold them onto the ceiling, so I always add a cable tie through each hole for added safety.

Papier mâché nest

You can make an excellent nest by covering a balloon with papier mâché . You can even add a little entrance tunnel. Cut one side off to make it sit level, hang it up, or let it roll and watch the rats discover the way in.

You will need

- Sheets of newspaper or phonebook pages
- A balloon
- A paintbrush
- Pet safe glue (see page 6)
- A small weight (optional)
- Straight sided glass or tumbler (optional)

Step by step

1. Make a stand to hold the nest while you're working. I used some paper towel around the top of a glass with plastic food wrap over the top.

2. Blow up the balloon. It helps to use something to weigh it down so you don't have to hold it. I used a metal napkin ring held on with a peg.

3. Paint the newspaper with glue on both sides and stick it around the balloon. Take the paper down the sides of the glass to hold the balloon in place.

4. Continue to wrap strips of newspaper around the balloon until you have three or four layers.

5. Leave to dry. Don't put it in the sun, as this will cause the air in the balloon to expand and weaken the papier mâché.

6. Repeat this until you have built up a thick layer of newspaper. The limiting factor is your own patience.

7. Ease the nest off the glass and pop the balloon to remove it.

8. You can trim the edges and cover it with plain paper to give a more finished look. Thicker paper will need more time for the glue to soak in before you smooth it onto the nest.

Hanging Cube

This makes a 20cm (8") cube with a door at each corner.

You will need

- 4 pieces of fabric, 75 cm x 25 cm (30 x 10")
- 2 square pieces of fabric 25cm x 25cm (10" x 10")
- 40 cm (16") of fixing strip (see page 5)
- 4 D rings

Step by step

1. Cut four pieces of fixing strip, each about 10 cm (4") long, and thread a D ring onto each strip.

2. Place one of the square pieces of fabric right side up, with the fixings placed diagonally in the corners.

3. Place the second square piece on top, right side down, and sew the layers together, leaving a gap to turn it right side out. Stitch diagonally across the fixings in the corners.

4. Turn right side out and stitch around the edges, then stitch across the layers to quilt the two layers of fabric together.

5. Use the other four pieces of fabric to make two more rectangles, but without the D ring fixings.

6. Lay the two long rectangles across each other, forming a cross.

7. Sew a triangle into each corner of the overlap to fix them together.

8. Sew the ends of the cross to the four edges of the square hammock, leaving the four sides open for ratty access. (You don't have to sew right to the corners if the layers are getting too thick for your machine).

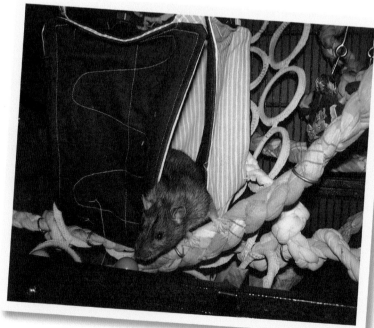

The sorting hat

This makes a swinging hat/hut with a round base and a pointed top.

You will need

- Three D rings
- A plate or round object to use as a template, around 20 to 25 cm (8 to 10").
- Some plastic needlepoint canvas, or other stiff material.
- Fabric. The size you need depends on the size of your plate/template. It needs to be 4 x the template diameter by 3 x the template diameter.
- Some newspaper, and possibly some tape to make a large enough sheet.

Step by step

1. Use the template to mark out and cut a circle in the plastic needlepoint canvas.

2. Fold the fabric in half, bringing the two shorter edges together.

3. Put the template about 2.5 cm (1") from the edge of the bottom corner of your fabric and draw around it.

4. Mark about 2.5 cm (1") outside the lines to give you a seam allowance, then cut through both layers to give you two circles of fabric.

5. To make a template for the side pieces, take a piece of newspaper at least 2 plates x 2 plates, and use a piece of string or a ruler to measure a quarter circle from one corner, two plate widths across.

6. Pin the newspaper on the folded fabric, with a straight edge along the fold and a straight edge along one edge of the fabric, and cut along the curved edge.

7. Open out the fabric into a semi circle. Fold one edge over to measure out three roughly equal pieces, and cut into three.

8. Fold each segment in half, right sides together, and machine sew around <u>all three</u> edges leaving a gap on the open straight edge to turn it right side out. Cut the points off the corners to help them turn out neatly.

9. Turn right side out and top stitch around the straight edges. Quilt together to discourage chewing.

10. Take the two circular pieces and sew together, about halfway between the line you first drew and the edge and leaving about 10 cm (4") gap to turn it through.

11. Cut notches around the seam allowance to reduce the bulk around the edge, then turn it right side out.

12. Check that the stiffening material is still a cm or so (0.4") smaller than the fabric circle, and if not then trim it down. Curl it up, post it in through the turning hole and work it into place.

11-12.

13. Hand sew up the hole and machine stitch around the edges to hold the stiffening in the centre of the circle. If you have used plastic needlepoint canvas you should be able to machine sew across the shape as well, to make it more chew resistant.

13.

14. Sew the curved edges of the three side pieces around the edge of the circle. The seams will stay on the outside to reduce chewing opportunities.

14.

15. Thread the top point of each piece through a D ring and sew in place.

15.

16. Hang all three D rings from the same fixing, using a trigger clip so that it can rotate.

Tubes & Tunnels

Rats love tunnels to lounge in or scamper through; in fact more often than not the problem is getting them out again. Here are a few tunnel ideas to start you off.

Scrounger's solution

Ask your local carpet shop if they have any centre tubes from rolls of carpet, or scrounge offcuts from the workers digging up your road.

Trouser tunnel

This idea uses a pair of toddler sized fleece trousers. If you don't have a toddler to deprive of their trousers, check out the charity shops. Just thread a couple of perches, ropes or chains in through the waist and out through the legs The legs can be fixed on different levels to make tunnel ramps. Add fixings to clip the legs to the chain if they slide along.

Knotted tunnel

Tie a long length of tumble dryer ducting in a knot. Tie it around something solid, or put it into a cardboard box and stuff the box with shredded paper to support the tunnel, and off you go.

Papier mâché tunnel

This is a fun way to make a tunnel for your rats, and is an ideal project for children. It can be as thick and strong as you have the patience to make it.

You will need

- Sheets of newspaper
- An empty 2 litre pop bottle
- A paintbrush
- Pet safe glue (see page 6)

Step by step

1. Cut off the top and bottom of the pop bottle to make a tube that is about the same diameter all the way down. Mind your fingers!

2. Cut or tear a sheet of newspaper or an old phonebook page into long thin strips.

3. Paint the newspaper with glue on both sides, and wrap it around the tube.

4. Continue to wrap strips of newspaper around the tube until you have three or four layers.

5. Leave to dry.

6. Repeat steps 4 and 5 until you have built up a thick layer of newspaper.

7. Compress the plastic tube to allow you to pull it out (or leave it inside for a water resistant lining) and cut off the ragged ends.

8. If required, add some more layers of newspaper over the cut edges to make a nice smooth edge.

9. You can cover it with plain paper inside and out to give a more finished look. If you're using good quality paper the glue will need more time to soak in before you smooth the strips on.

10. Allow to dry fully and then give it to your rats to destroy, **OR** make six of them and use more papier mâché to fix them together into a pyramid.

New tunnel hammock from old jeans

This is a fairly quick and simple way to turn a pair of old jeans into a sturdy tunnel, although I will warn that they seem to be quite tasty too.

You will need

- A pair of old jeans
- 4 D rings
- 40 cm (16") of fixing strip (see page 5)
- A heavy or denim needle fitted to your sewing machine.

Step by step

1. If the bottom edges of the jeans are frayed, trim off the frayed edges and re-turn the hem.

2. Put your hand down one leg of the jeans from the top, grab hold of the bottom of both legs and pull one leg of the jeans up through the other. It helps later if the seams are not completely lined up inside.

3. Cut through all four layers near the top of the leg, but below any tears or worn seams.

4. Cut four pieces of handle strip, each about 10 cm (4") long, and thread a D ring onto each one.

5. Fold the strip back around a D ring and put it ring first between two layers of the top of the leg, with the strip about 2 cm (0.8") into the seam. Add another D ring about 10 cm (4") along.

6. Sew around the top of the leg through two layers, taking the sewing machine foot as close to the D ring inside as you can. The shorter the strip, the harder to chew. Add in the second D ring a little less than halfway round.

7. Sew around again a small distance apart from the first line to add strength to the seam.

8. Turn the fabric the right way out and sew around the same edge again, close to the edge if your machine will cope with the thickness, further away if not.

9. At the other end of the leg add two more D rings, but this time with the ring sticking out. Try to line them up with those at the first end, and put them fairly snugly into the edge to foil the chewers.

10. Sew around this edge just behind the hem.

11. Now get your machine foot inside the tube and sew the two layers together up and down inside the leg. Get as far in as possible from each end as the more the two layers are sewn together the less likely the ratties are to get between the layers. Mind your fingers!

12. Cut off any loose threads, and your tunnel hammock is now ready to hang.

Cloth tunnel

You don't have to butcher a pair of jeans to make a tunnel. This version is based on the basic hammock. If you're sewing for large bucks, increase the size from 40 cm to 50 cm (16" to 20"). You can also add more layers of fabric if you want to make it stronger.

You will need

- 2 pieces of fabric about 2.5 cm (1") longer than you want the finished tunnel to be, and about 40 cm (16") wide.
- 40 cm (16") of fixing strip (see page 5)
- 4 x D rings

Step by step

1. Make a plain and simple hammock, as shown on page 31, but with the fixing rings on the 40 cm (16") edges about 5 cm (2") from the corners.

2. Fold the hammock over with the fixing rings at the ends and the lining material on the outside and sew the two long edges together.

3. Turn right side out.

4. Sew down the seams on the inside to discourage chewing.

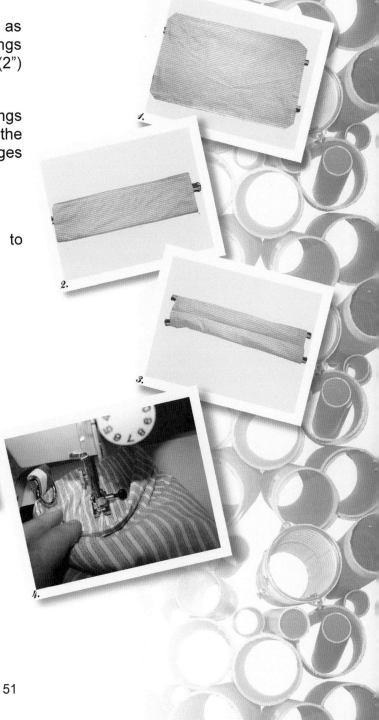

Cuddling & Carrying

Rats love to be with you. They're an incredibly interactive pet, especially for their small size. Here are some ideas to help you carry them safely and securely.

In your clothes

Your rats will love to burrow in your clothes and hide in your sleeves, or nestle under your hair. Hoods are an excellent place for a nap. If your top isn't too slippery they may like to ride on your shoulder too.

In a handbag

An old handbag or shoulder bag can make a really unobtrusive yet comfortable carrier for your ratties.

In a sports bag inside a carrier.

Some small pet carriers fit comfortably inside shoulder sports bags, giving a useful way to keep your rats warm and away from the weather if you have to carry them to visit the vet.

Hamster cage carrier

Although there are a number of specially designed small pet carriers on the market, if you are travelling any distance or have several rats you may be better off with a small hamster cage. It is easier to fit a water bottle and you can provide a small hammock for them to lounge in. Watch the small ads in your local paper for a low cost second hand cage.

Sock buddy

A rat's favourite thing to cuddle up to is another rat. If your rat has been left on his or her own and circumstances mean you absolutely can't get another companion, a sock buddy or two can help ease their loneliness. Just ball up a few old socks together and put it into their nest with them.

Beanie pouch

Use a close-knit or fleece hat to make a carry pouch. Either add some cord to hang it round your neck, or attach it to an old sweatshirt with a few stitches or some safety pins.

Carry pouch

Many rats will happily hide in a rat pouch that hangs around your neck, especially if they get used to it from a young age, and it makes a fun way to carry them around and bond with you. It's very simple to make, but here is the way I do it. If your fabrics have a right side, the instructions will tell you which way up to place them. If they don't, then it doesn't matter which way up you place them.

You will need

- Outer fabric and lining fabric, each around 35 cm (14") x 50 cm (20").
- 100 cm (40") of fixing strip (see page 5)
- 2 D rings

Step by step

1. Cut two pieces of handle strip, each about 10 cm (4") long, and thread a D ring onto each strip.

2. Place one piece of fabric right side up and place the two fixing strips on one of the shorter sides about 3.5 cm (1.5") from the corners, so that about 1 cm (0.4") of the strip shows. Sew across the end to hold them in place.

3. Put the second piece of fabric on top, right side down.

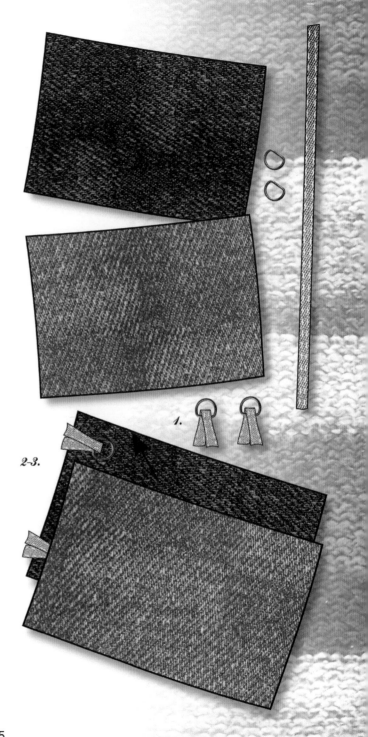

4. Sew around the edges about 1 to 1.5 cm (0.4 to 0.6") from the edge, leaving a 8 to 10 cm (3 to 4") gap unsewn to let you turn the hammock right side out.

5. Trim the hem across at the corners.

6. Turn the pouch right side out through the hole and hand sew the hole together.

7. Stitch around the edges and then stitch over the two layers to quilt them together and make the pouch more chew resistant.

8. Fold in half and machine sew up the sides.

9. Use the remaining fixing strip to make a neck strap of a comfortable length. Zigzag across the unfinished ends of the strap to neaten them.

Hoodie pouch

This rat pouch is modelled on the front pocket of a hoodie, the sort that lets you put your hands in both sides. The rats seem to love being able to pop their heads out of the two sides.

You will need

- Outer fabric and lining fabric, each around 35 x 50 cm (14 x 20").
- 100 cm (40") of fixing strip (see page 5)
- 2 D rings

Step by step

1. Cut two pieces of fixing strip, each about 10 cm (4") long, and thread a D ring onto each strip.

2. At one end, measure about 10 cm (4") from each corner in both directions and draw across the corner, then cut the corner off along the lines.

3. Place one piece of fabric right side up and place the two fixing strips at the uncut end, 3.5 cm (1.5") from the corners, so that about 1 cm (0.4") of the strip shows. Sew across the end to hold them in place.

4. Put the second piece of fabric on top, right side down.

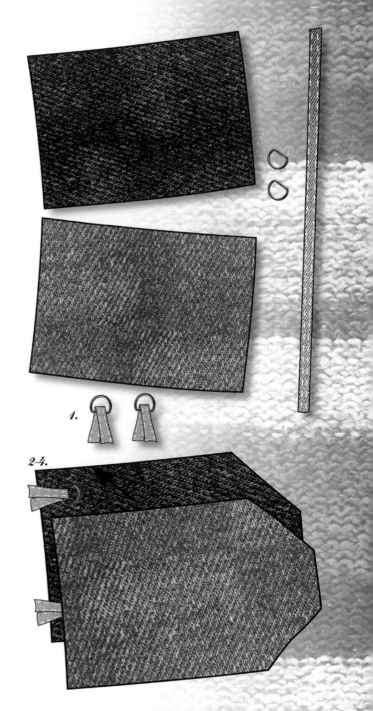

5-6.

8.

9.

10.

5. Sew around the edges about 1 to 1.5 cm (0.4 to 0.6") from the edge, leaving an 8 to 10 cm (3 to 4") gap unsewn to turn the hammock right side out through.

6. Trim the seams across at the corners.

7. Turn the pouch right side out through the hole and hand sew the hole together.

8. Stitch around the edges and then stitch over the two layers to quilt them together and make the pouch more chew resistant.

9. Fold in half and machine sew up the sides and across the middle edge at the top.

10. Use the remaining fixing strip to make a neck strap of a comfortable length. Zigzag across the unfinished ends of the strap to neaten them.

Rat sling

I love my rat sling. It came about because I wanted to able to move about more without a bag around my neck swinging out, and I was looking for a way to make it more like a handbag, but still be really secure and have plenty of room.

You will need

- Lining fabric at least 80 x 65 cm (32 x 26")
- Outer fabric at least 80 x 100 cm (32 x 40")
- Paper/tissue to copy the pattern onto.

Step by step

1. Cut a strip for the shoulder strap about 15 cm (6") wide and 100 cm (40") long from the longest edge of the outer fabric.

2. Photocopy and enlarge the sling pattern on the next page, or draw a 2.5 cm (1") grid onto a sheet of paper, and copy the pattern across square by square.

3. Fold your outer fabric in half with the two shorter edges together.

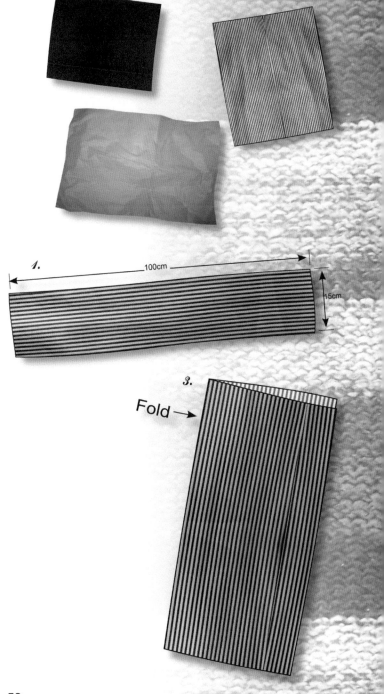

I've tried to avoid templates, but this is the only way I could see to give you this one. It is symmetrical top to bottom, so you only need to copy across the top half and then fold it to trace the bottom half. The pattern is also online at

www.rattycorner.com/handbook

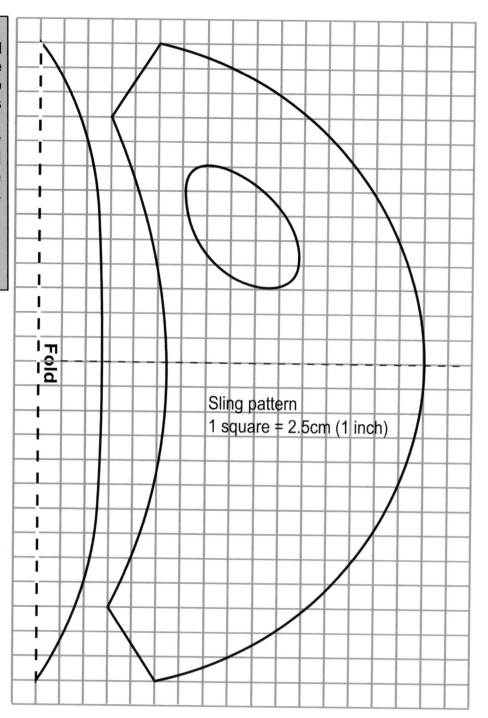

Fold

Sling pattern
1 square = 2.5cm (1 inch)

60

4. Pin your pattern onto the fabric with the smaller shape running along the fold of the material.

5. Cut out the pieces, but don't cut the hole at this stage. The lines on the pattern are the cutting line, not the sewing line.

6. Re-use the pattern pieces to cut the lining. Again, don't cut out the hole yet. You don't need a handle strip from this fabric, just the three pieces.

7. Your sling will hang over one shoulder, with the hole up towards that shoulder. Decide which shoulder you would like your sling to hang from. I prefer to have the sling over my right shoulder so that it's easier to put my right hand in through the hole.

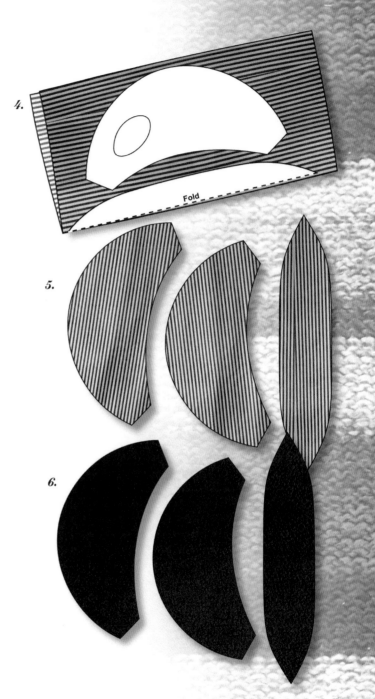

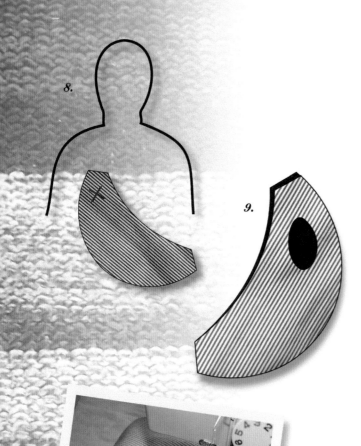

8. Your outer fabric will probably have a 'right' side - the side that you want to be on the outside of your sling. Hold one of the two matching outer pieces up against yourself with the right side of the fabric facing **away** from you. You can then see which end of the piece will be up towards your shoulder - stick a pin in to mark it. Place the pattern back on the cloth and cut out the hole at the end with the pin.

9. Pin the piece with the hole on top of the matching piece of fleece, with the right sides of the fabric together and the wrong side of the outer fabric facing you. Do not cut a hole in the fleece yet.

10. Sew around the hole about 7 or 8 mm (0.3") from the edge, and only then cut the matching hole into the fleece fabric.

11. Cut notches around the edge, close to but not through the stitching.

12. Turn the material right side out through the hole and then top stitch around the hole.

13. Stitch around the edge of the two pieces of material, fixing the outer layer to the lining with right sides out. Sew around the edge of the second side and the base, again with right sides outward.

14. It makes the sling much more chew resistant if you now add some stitching to quilt the outer and lining pieces together across the whole area. With this stripey material you could sew back and forth along the stripes to make it less obvious.

15. Take the base piece and place it on the long edge of one of the sides, right sides together and an equal distance from each end of the side piece. Sew them together about 1cm (0.4") from the edge with the stitching starting and ending about 1cm (0.4") short of the pointed ends of the base.

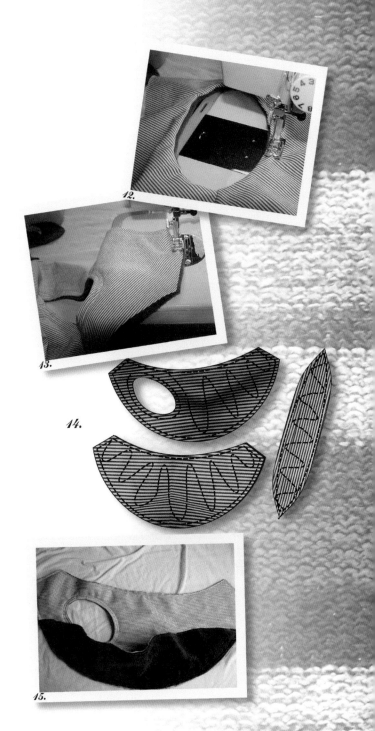

12.

13.

14.

15.

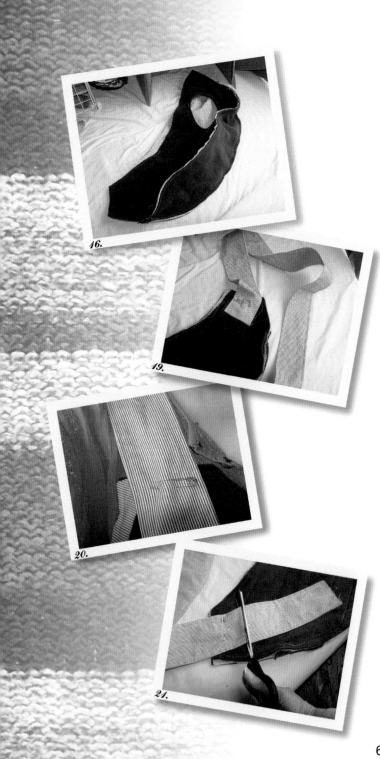

16. Now sew the second side to the base, again stopping short of the points of the base.

17. Take the long strip of material you cut for the handle, fold it lengthways with the wrong side out, and sew up the long side about 1cm from the edge. Leave the two ends open.

18. Pull this through itself until it is right side out. Top stitch along its length about 5mm from each edge.

19. Pin the ends of the handle to the two ends of the sling. It doesn't matter which side, we're just working out the length at present.

20. Put the sling on and adjust the handle to the length you'd like it.

21. Trim the ends, leaving a good length to sew in.

22. Now the tricky bit. Unpin your handle, and position it inside the sling between the two sides, with the same amount sticking out that you left earlier to sew in. Do the same at the other end, making sure the handle isn't twisted. Machine stitch them in place between the two side pieces.

23. Sew all around the open edges, making sure it's sewn together all around the top from the base point right round to the other base point, without catching the handle into the seam.

24. Turn right side out, through the entrance hole.

25. Now you need to top stitch the seams on the outside to hide the raw edges from the ratties inside the sling, and to add some rigidity. Sew one edge of the base, then reposition and sew along the second edge. Then reposition again and do the rest of the edges. You may have to leave a small gap near the base points if your machine can't cope with the thickness of the layers.

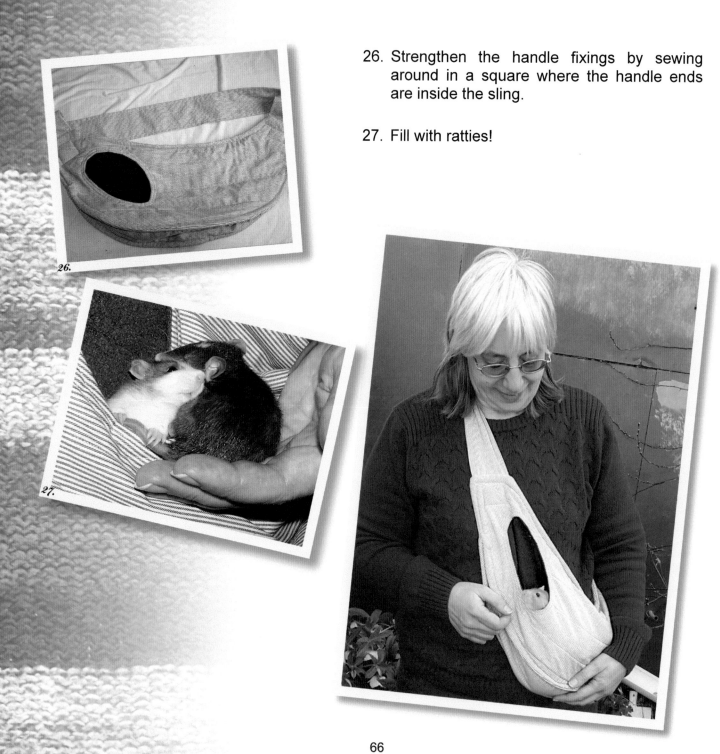

26. Strengthen the handle fixings by sewing around in a square where the handle ends are inside the sling.

27. Fill with ratties!

66

Places to Play

Your rats will enjoy being allowed out of their cage each day to interact with you and explore their environment. The area needs to be made safe, with no cables to chew or places to injure themselves. They also have a taste for remote control/phone buttons.

On the table

A table can be a handy place to let your rats play without giving them the run of a room. Rats are much more sensible about not jumping down than some other small rodents. Cover the table with a waterproof sheet or cut some old cushion flooring to size, and then add toys and rats.

In the hallway

If your household isn't constantly in and out of the hallway, this can give you a room without wires and tempting hidey holes.

In the bathroom

Again, the bathroom gives you a place without wires and usually with an easily wipeable floor. Make sure there are no holes next to pipes that they can disappear into, and remember to keep the toilet lid down.

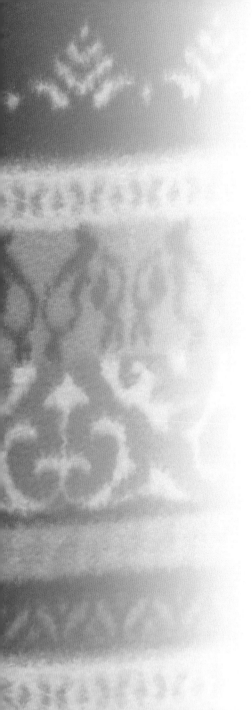

On your bed

Some rats (not mine, I'm afraid) are good enough to stay on your bed to play. Cover your bed with a thick blanket to protect your covers, and be prepared for the inexplicable holes that may appear.

In the living room

You can just put up with the mess they make and let them loose in your living room. Move any wires out of the way or use trunking to protect them and make sure there are no holes in the base of your furniture they can disappear into. Beware of holes in your sofa – if there are none to start with, they may appear spontaneously.

In a playpen

An alternative to the table is to build a playpen for the rats – basically a wall to keep them in. Keep in mind that they can jump very well, so the height needs to be at least 75 cm. If you want to be able to get in there with them, which is the ideal, then it also needs to be short enough for you to step over and large enough that you can't be used as a jumping off point for escape. Cardboard won't hold ratties for long, so the simplest way is to use hardboard or corrugated plastic, hinged with strong tape, and with an overlap that you can wedge or clip together.

My first ratty playpen was made from old cage panels cable tied together and covered with thick plastic sheeting; not very pretty, but it did the job until they chewed the sheeting off.

In their own rat room

This is the ideal, if you have the space. Giving the rats their own room means you can just open the cage and let them out to play. From experience they are still safer with supervision, but if there is space to set your own toys out too it can become your refuge as well.

In the cage

The majority of rats spend most of their time in their cage, so it's important as a place to play. I hate to see a bare, tidy cage with very little for the rats to do, preferring to have a cage packed full of activities. Our pets are much, much smaller than we are and what looks like a crowded space to us is interesting and enriching to them. As long as there's space for them to stretch, climb, and jump then their cage isn't too full.

Choose a bigger cage if you can; *at least* 50 x 50 x 80 cm (20 x 20 x 36") for a pair of rats. There are quite often bargains on ebay or on pet forums, and your rats will appreciate having room to play within their cage.

Wheels

I wouldn't be without a wheel in each of my rat cages. Most rats will use a wheel if they are introduced to it at an early age, and it provides an opportunity for exercise which takes up very little space.

I have used Wobust Wodent Wheels and Large Silent Spinners in my cages, although there are other similar brands now available. Look for a wheel robust enough to hold the weight of your rats without tipping over, with no wire or parts that could trap their tails, and preferably that won't make so much noise that you have to take it out at night.

28091446R00041

Printed in Great Britain
by Amazon